I Learned to LEAN on Jesus
WITH FAITH IN ACTION

✝ faith books&MORE

Suwanee, Georgia

JUANITA COLLIER ZACKERY

First published by Faith Books & MORE
978-0-9852729-5-1

Printed in the United States of America.

This book is printed on acid-free paper.

faith books&MORE

3255 Lawrenceville-Suwanee Rd.
Suite P250
Suwanee, GA 30024
publishing@faithbooksandmore.com
www.faithbooksandmore.com

Dedication

I dedicate this book to Carolyn Johnson. She came to my work place and asked the director about volunteer work and she assigned her to me. I asked Carolyn if she would like to update our agency's resource list and she stated she would be glad to do so. I had completed writing my book as God instructed me and had no one to type it, nor help me further. I asked God to send me someone that will type my book and help me get it published. God spoke to me and said Carolyn is the one I have sent to type your book. I asked her and she gladly accepted the offer. She said she would stick with me until my book was ready to be published and she did just that. So a Very Special Thanks to God and to Carolyn for her dedicated work on my behalf.

A Note from the Author

This book content is based on faith and faith is the substance of things hoped for and the evidence of things not seen. As I, the author of this book encourages you to read the entire chapter of Hebrews 11:1-40, how faith defined and illustrated through Old Testament heroes. I have been blessed, hopefully you, too, will be blessed as you read the following true testimonies of my walk with God and a poem from when I first sought Jesus.

Hebrews 11:1-40

1 Now faith is the substance of things hoped for, the evidence of things not seen.

2 For by it the elders obtained a good report.

3 Through faith we understand that the worlds were framed by the word of God, so that things which are seen were not made of things which do appear.

4 By faith Abel offered unto God a more excellent sacrifice than Cain, by which he obtained witness that he was righteous, God testifying of his gifts: and by it he being dead yet speaketh.

5 By faith Enoch was translated that he should not see death; and was not found, because God had translated him: for before his translation he had this testimony, that he pleased God.

6 But without faith it is impossible to please him: for he that cometh to God must believe that he is, and that he is a rewarder of them that diligently seek him.

7 By faith Noah, being warned of God of things not seen as yet, moved with fear, prepared an ark to the saving of his house; by the which he condemned the world, and became heir of the righteousness which is by faith.

8 By faith Abraham, when he was called to go out into a place which he should after receive for an inheritance, obeyed; and he went out, not knowing whither he went.

9 By faith he sojourned in the land of promise, as in a strange country, dwelling in tabernacles with Isaac and Jacob, the heirs with him of the same promise:

10 For he looked for a city which hath foundations, whose builder and maker is God.

11 Through faith also Sara herself received strength to conceive seed, and was delivered of a child when she was past age, because she judged him faithful who had promised.

12 Therefore sprang there even of one, and him as good as dead, so many as the stars of the sky in multitude, and as the sand which is by the sea shore innumerable.

13 These all died in faith, not having received the promises, but having seen them afar off, and were persuaded of them, and embraced them, and confessed that they were strangers and pilgrims on the earth.

14 For they that say such things declare plainly that they seek a country.

15 And truly, if they had been mindful of that country from whence they came out, they might have had opportunity to have returned.

16 But now they desire a better country, that is, an heavenly: wherefore God is not ashamed to be called their God: for he hath prepared for them a city.

17 By faith Abraham, when he was tried, offered up Isaac: and he that had received the promises offered up his only begotten son,

18 Of whom it was said, That in Isaac shall thy seed be called:

19 Accounting that God was able to raise him up, even from the dead; from whence also he received him in a figure.

20 By faith Isaac blessed Jacob and Esau concerning things to come.

21 By faith Jacob, when he was a dying, blessed both the sons of Joseph; and worshipped, leaning upon the top of his staff.

22 By faith Joseph, when he died, made mention of the departing of the children of Israel; and gave commandment concerning his bones.

23 By faith Moses, when he was born, was hid three months of his parents, because they saw he was a proper child; and they were not afraid of the king's commandment.

24 By faith Moses, when he was come to years, refused to be called the son of Pharaoh's daughter;

25 Choosing rather to suffer affliction with the people of God, than to enjoy the pleasures of sin for a season;

26 Esteeming the reproach of Christ greater riches than the treasures in Egypt: for he had respect unto the recompence of the reward.

27 By faith he forsook Egypt, not fearing the wrath of the king: for he endured, as seeing him who is invisible.

28 Through faith he kept the passover, and the sprinkling of blood, lest he that destroyed the firstborn should touch them.

29 By faith they passed through the Red sea as by dry land: which the Egyptians assaying to do were drowned.

30 By faith the walls of Jericho fell down, after they were compassed about seven days.

31 By faith the harlot Rahab perished not with them that believed not, when she had received the spies with peace.

32 And what shall I more say? for the time would fail me to tell of Gedeon, and of Barak, and of Samson, and of Jephthae; of David also, and Samuel, and of the prophets:

33 Who through faith subdued kingdoms, wrought righteousness, obtained promises, stopped the mouths of lions.

34 Quenched the violence of fire, escaped the edge of the sword, out of weakness were made strong, waxed valiant in fight, turned to flight the armies of the aliens.

35 Women received their dead raised to life again: and others were tortured, not accepting deliverance; that they might obtain a better resurrection:

36 And others had trial of cruel mockings and scourgings, yea, moreover of bonds and imprisonment:

37 They were stoned, they were sawn asunder, were tempted, were slain with the sword: they wandered about in sheepskins and goatskins; being destitute, afflicted, tormented;

38 (Of whom the world was not worthy:) they wandered in deserts, and in mountains, and in dens and caves of the earth.

39 And these all, having obtained a good report through faith, received not the promise:

40 God having provided some better thing for us, that they without us should not be made perfect.

Introduction

In early May 1953, a sanctified woman preacher named Mother Margaret Sutton from Cordele, Georgia came to Montezuma, Georgia to conduct a revival in a Methodist Church. She taught about holiness and against sin. The more she taught, the more I understood that I didn't have salvation according to the Word. There was much sin in my heart for which I needed to repent, but because I was young I wanted to wait and do what I wanted to do until I became an adult and got married. God said differently, however. Mother Sutton made an altar call. I felt that going up for prayer couldn't hurt anything. I still planned to wait until I was grown to receive the Holy Ghost. But when I went to the altar and fell on my knees for prayer, I was unable to get up. I began to seek God for the Holy Ghost.

I prayed and sought God for several nights. I felt as Paul did when he wrote in Romans 7:24, "O' wretched man that I am; who shall deliver me from the body of this death?" On June 7, 1953, at the age of fourteen, as I was about to start the ninth grade and enter high school, Jesus came into my life. He saved, sanctified, and filled me with the Holy Ghost. At the First Born Church of a Living God in Fort Valley, Georgia, El Shaddai, the Almighty God delivered me. I was filled with the Holy Ghost according to Acts 2:3-4 and received the power spoken of in Acts 1:8.

So I began to lean on Jesus. He meant everything to me. As I kept going to school, my faith grew stronger in God's work, believing that He would do just what His Word said He would do. When I saw someone sick in my class or around the school I would offer to pray for their condition and the Lord would heal them. In my walk with God, I had several experiences which taught me to lean on Jesus with "Faith in Action."

Come unto me, all ye that labour and are heavy laden, and I will give you rest. Take my yoke upon you, and learn of me; for I am meek and lowly in heart: and ye shall find rest unto your souls. For my yoke is easy, and my burden is light.

Matthew 11:28-30 (KJV)

Contents

Come unto me, all ye that labour and are heavy laden, and I will give you rest. Take my yoke upon you, and learn of me; for I am meek and lowly in heart: and ye shall find rest unto your souls. For my yoke is easy, and my burden is light.

Matthew 11:28-30 (KJV)

CHAPTER

1

Jesus' Delivering Power

Come unto me, all ye that labour and are heavy laden, and I will give you rest. Take my yoke upon you, and learn of me; for I am meek and lowly in heart: and ye shall find rest unto your souls. For my yoke is easy, and my burden is light.
Matthew 11:28-30 (KJV)

Early in my relationship with Him, I recognized God as El Shaddai, the Almighty God, and the Deliverer. Throughout the Word this name reveals and emphasizes God's power to deliver His people out of the hands of their enemies. It shows His all-sufficiency and almighty power, the supreme power over all. The almighty, all-powerful, all-sufficient God was manifested in Jesus' body when He raised Him from the dead. As you read my testimonies that follow, I hope you can see what a powerful deliverer El Shaddai has been for me.

When the devil saw how sincere and faithful to God I was (e.g. attending every prayer service, every bible study class, etc.), he tried to stop me and my sister, Doris, through our father, who was not yet saved. He commanded us not to go back to church and to stop the way we praised and worshipped God. He stated that when we prayed we could be heard five miles away and it didn't take all that to serve God.

Doris and I began to talk to each other and expressed how much we loved Jesus and how we couldn't give up serving the Lord. We decided to go on a three-day fast with sincere prayer to get the victory over Satan. The third day of the fast, on a Sunday morning, we began to pray, praise God, and wait for an answer. All of a sudden, we heard our father walking back and forth outside our bedroom. He seemed very disturbed and distressed. Then, as if he couldn't hold it in any longer, he cried out, "Children! Children! Ain't you going to church this morning?"

"Daddy," we called, "we wanted to go, but you told us we could not go back to church. The people that usually pick us up are not coming."

"It's alright," our father answered. "Just get ready. I'll take you myself from now on."

He explained that he had thought Holiness was right, but that no one could really live holy. "You all have proven to me you can live Holy," he said.

Not only did our father take us to church that day; he went to the altar, repented of his sins, gave his heart to Jesus, and was filled with the Holy Ghost. Later he began to preach the gospel. Several others of our siblings were saved and baptized with the Holy Ghost, speaking in tongues as the Spirit of God gave them utterance. That was truly faith in action. That was when I recognized God as El Shaddai, the Almighty God; "El Shaddai, my deliverer."

I had just recently been saved when, as a fourteen-year-old new member of the First Born Church of a Living God in Fort Valley, Georgia, my church sent me off to convocation in Waycross, Georgia. I had never been away from home before. But I tried to be brave. After placing me in a nice room at Ms. Mary Lee Lane's home, the couple I had been traveled with informed me they were going on to Jacksonville, Florida, and they would see me in two days. That didn't really concern me because I felt confident I would be able to walk to the church and back alone without any problems.

The next morning, Ms. Mary Lee walked me to the church for service. But when I started back to her house it seemed as though all the streets and all the houses looked just alike. I had made the mistake of not carrying the address with me and I couldn't remember Ms. Mary Lee's last name. I kept walking up and down one street after another. I got so confused I didn't know my way back to the church and I couldn't remember its address. I started to cry. I began to pray and ask God to lead me to Ms. Mary Lee's house.

I cannot tell you how I got there, but when I came to myself, I was on Ms. Mary Lee's porch knocking on the door. I believe I was caught up in the Spirit of the Lord and an angel led me there. I praised God for another miracle of faith in action.

Another time, I travelled to Miami, Florida, alone on a Trailways bus. On the return trip, I got off the bus in South Bay, Florida, to use the restroom. The driver had said it was no problem because he was going to Belle Glade to pick up passengers then he would return. But I had a serious problem. I'd left my purse containing my phone book, my money, and my ticket on the seat where I had been sitting. I had nothing with me.

Thank God for Jesus. I began to pray and ask God to not let anyone touch my purse. When the bus returned, I was the first one in line to get back on. Praise God, my purse and all my belonging were there just as I'd left them. He had preserved them. Praise God for His miracle-working power with faith in action.

Once when I was on my job with the Head Start program, all the staff had left except me and two coworkers, one of whom had accidentally locked her purse in her desk drawer. We didn't know how she was going to get her purse without calling a locksmith. It was getting late—nearly dark—and she kept trying to open the drawer with other keys. Nothing worked. Finally, she asked me to come over and see what I could do.

I had witnessed God open a locked luggage before when one of my sisters lost her keys. So, talking to Jesus in my heart, I went over to the drawer. Reaching my right hand toward it, I said, "In the name of Jesus—"

Without my hand touching it and without a key, the power of the Living God opened that drawer. Nothing else opened except the drawer that contained her purse. All the other drawers stayed locked. She had to use the key that was in her purse to open the other drawers. Praise God! What a miracle; another example of faith in action.

With one of my pregnancies, I was often aggravated. All the while I carried that child I was disagreeable. After she was born, she was a beautiful child, but she was very mean and disagreeable and it was so hard to please her. No one else could hold her or keep her so I had to deal with her all the time. I dealt with this problem until she was three years old.

The next child that came was such a good baby; peaceful and calm.

I learned a lesson about attitudes from that experience. My daughter was so mean and evil. She could not play with other children. I recognized that she was being tormented by an evil spirit and Satan was trying to take possession of her even at such a young age.

One morning I prepared myself spiritually to deal with her. When she got up, that evil spirit in her started acting up; more contrary than ever. I went to my front door, opened it wide, and told the devil to get out of my house and not to come back. I said, "I command you in the name of Jesus not to torment this child anymore." I stood my ground and told Satan he had to leave because we were not going to pay rent for him to live in our house any longer.

That morning, he left out my front door. Ever since, my daughter has been in perfect peace, able to play and communicate with other children. Praise God for His miracle-working power! That was another example of faith in action.

We had a prayer group that met at our house. One night, while everyone was praying, one of the members was holding my baby, Alfred. We had a fan running to keep the room cool. We really got into deep meditative prayer. Suddenly, I heard a loud noise from the fan. I got up off my knees to see what was wrong with it. I saw that the baby had stuck his right hand into the fan. I quickly cut off the fan.

I was afraid to look at the baby's hand. But when I examined it closely, there was no injury to be found, not even scratches. With my prayer group, I praised God for his miracle-working power; another example of faith in action.

Come unto me, all ye that labour and are heavy laden, and I will give you rest. Take my yoke upon you, and learn of me; for I am meek and lowly in heart: and ye shall find rest unto your souls. For my yoke is easy, and my burden is light.

Matthew 11:28-30 (KJV)

CHAPTER

2

Jesus' Healing Power

Come unto me, all ye that labour and are heavy laden, and I will give you rest. Take my yoke upon you, and learn of me; for I am meek and lowly in heart: and ye shall find rest unto your souls. For my yoke is easy, and my burden is light.

Matthew 11:28-30 (KJV)

CHAPTER

2

Jesus' Healing Power

Come unto me, all ye that labour and are heavy laden, and I will give you rest. Take my yoke upon you, and learn of me; for I am meek and lowly in heart: and ye shall find rest unto your souls. For my yoke is easy, and my burden is light.

Matthew 11:28-30 (KJV)

After experiencing such miraculously healings, I began to recognize the name Jehovah Rophi: "The Lord is a Healer." God identified himself to the children of Israel as their Healer. He said, "I am the Lord (Jehovah Rophi) that healeth thee" (Exodus 15:26).

Jesus manifested, revealed, and made known God's name, Jehovah Rophi, as he went from village to village healing all manner of diseases. He opened blinded eyes, restored hearing, made the lame walk, and healed all who were oppressed of the devil. Still today, Jesus is our healer. "By His stripes we are healed" (Isaiah 53:5). As you read these healing testimonies you will see what the name Jehovah Rophi has meant to me.

Early in my walk with Jesus, sanctification and holiness were not widespread in our little town of Montezuma, Georgia. People called those who got saved, sanctified, and filled with the Holy Ghost "Holy Rollers." They would make fun of us for shouting and speaking in tongues.

The school bus driver, Mr. Charlie Dean, didn't know Jesus. I was riding the bus one day when this man had the whole bus full of students laughing about my religion. I warned him not to blaspheme against the Holy Ghost, but He kept on.

Shortly afterward, a pain hit him. He became too sick to drive and stopped the bus. The students began yelling at him, concerned that they were going to be late for school. He said, "I am very sick. I can't continue. Ask Juanita to come up and pray for me."

"God is not to be played with," I informed Mr. Dean. "If you don't know what you are talking about you need to keep your mouth shut. But I am going to pray that God will forgive and heal you." I laid my hands on the man and asked God to forgive him for his ignorance and to heal his body.

Immediately, the Lord healed him. He was able to finish his school route that morning and Mr. Dean never made any more jokes again about me serving God. Praise God for His miracle-working power. That was another miracle of faith in action.

Once I had boils as big as medium eggs rise up under my arms. An evangelist from Alabama, Bishop Perry Thomas, came to our church for a week-long revival. He was a man of great faith. The night I attended he preached from Luke 7:11-19 about the ten lepers. He talked about his experience with trusting God. He made an altar call and I went up for prayer.

After Bishop Thomas prayed for me, as I was heading home, the devil whispered in my ears. He said, "Just put some baking soda under your arms and everything will be alright." As soon as I got home, I put the baking soda under my arms. It cooked those boils like you would cook a pot of meat. I was so miserable and disgusted for listening to the devil. I told the Lord I realized I had done wrong.

The word of the Lord spoke to me from Hebrew 11:6, the latter part of that verse. "For him that cometh to God must believe that He is and that He is a rewarder of them that diligently seek him." I repented and said, "Lord, what should I do?"

The Spirit spoke to me and told me, "Go back and get prayer

again." So I went back the next night and told the Bishop what had happened. I asked him to pray for me again and he did. I was instantly healed and all the soreness and pain left my arms, another miracle of faith in action.

There was a time when I had a lot of problems with my tonsils. During flare-ups, they would swell, my throat would get so sore I couldn't swallow, and I would have a very high fever. I took a lot of pain pills, but they would not work so I would go to Grady Hospital to get antibiotics to help with the problem.

One night my throat became sore and I had the highest fever. I decided I was not going to take anything for the condition anymore. I gave the problem to Jesus, according to the pattern found in 1 Peter 5:7, "Casting all your care upon Him for He careth for you." So I went to bed, burning up with fever. I prayed, "Lord, here I am. It seems as if man can't cure this problem. I don't want to have my tonsils taken out, so I'm leaving it all up to you."

Finally, I drifted off to sleep. In the wee hours of the morning, just before the break of day, I felt a cool breeze come over my body. Jesus came in and took away all the fever, the soreness, and the swelling of my tonsils. I was miraculously healed and I have never had a problem with my tonsils again. Praise God for His miracle-working power and another example of faith in action.

One of my daughters, Valerie, was born knock-kneed. When she began to walk, her knees knocked together and her feet turned inward. I was told I must take her to Emory Children's Hospital for braces before she turned four years of age, before the bones set so that they could not be straightened. Valerie was already three years of age, so I didn't have much time to waste.

As soon as I made up my mind to take her, Jesus spoke to me and said, "Haven't you seen my miracle-working power?"

I said, "Yes, Lord."

Immediately, I got my anointing oil, picked up the child, laid her across my lap, anointed her knees, legs, and feet with the oil, and began to pray. I asked God in the name of Jesus to straighten Valerie's knees and legs, making them normal, as they were supposed to be, and we would give him all the praise. Right before my very eyes a miracle was performed. Her knees and feet instantly straightened and they have been normal ever since. I never made it to Emory. That was another miracle of faith in action.

After giving birth to my eighth child, I became anemic. I had to take iron tablets and eat a lot of certain foods that could build up my blood. I stayed tired all the time. In the apartment where we lived, the bedrooms were upstairs. If I had to go upstairs to get something I would need to rest before coming back downstairs. A nurse at the Health Department kept me supplied with iron tablets.

One day I was on the phone with a friend. We started talking about trusting God for my healing. When I got off the phone I went out to pick up something for dinner. While walking to the store, I heard a voice say, "One of these days you are going to stretch out on faith. What's wrong with today?"

So I said, "Yes, Lord."

"If you believe me for healing," He said, "throw every one of those pills in the garbage and trust me for your deliverance."

When I got home, I threw all my medication out.

The devil started talking to me. "What are you going to do now that you threw away all your pills?" he said. "Well, you can eat some rare liver, drink sweet milk, eat plenty of beets, lots of green vegetables, and drink grape juice."

I answered, "Satan, I rebuke you in the name of Jesus. I don't need any of your advice on how I should eat. I am not going to eat any of those foods because Jesus has healed me and He doesn't need any help."

Later, tests at the clinic showed I was completely healed of low blood pressure and anemia. Praise God for His wonder-working power bringing me a miracle of faith in action.

Another time I was suffering from hemorrhoids. I'd tried many ointments for relief, but the problem persisted. One day I was listening to A.A. Allen's radio broadcast. A lady testified how God had healed her hemorrhoid condition. So I threw up my hands and cried, "Jesus, if you did it for her, surely you can do it for me."

Immediately, I felt a cool breeze run from my rectum up my spine. I was instantly healed of that condition. I began to praise and magnify God for another miracle of faith in action.

At about ten years of age, one of my sons began to have seizures. Most of the episodes would happen at school, but sometimes he would have one at home. My husband and I would pray and rebuke them.

We took him to Grady Hospital to see a doctor about the cause of the seizures. The doctor was unable to tell us why he was having them. He prescribed medication to help control them, but it was difficult getting the child to take it.

Even when he got old enough to go to high school, he was still having the seizures. They were not violent, but one day he brought home a note saying if we didn't get the condition under control they would have to put him out of school. He still would not take the medication.

"Devil," I said, "you have got to go." I began to pray earnestly and went on a three-day fast. I wore a handkerchief against my skin. After completing the fast, I took the handkerchief and pinned it on the clothes my son was wearing so it would be next to his body.

As in Acts 19:11-12, Jesus delivered him. The seizures left. He finished high school and the seizures never came back. Praise God for another miracle of faith in action.

When she came to the age of menstruation, one of my daughters had such severe pain each month that she would be unable to cope with it. One day she fell out of bed and began to roll on the floor, crying and screaming.

I got up and went to her room. I said, "Devil, I am tired of you tormenting my daughter with these painful monthly cycles. I command you, in the name of Jesus, to loose my daughter right now. I command that every pain leave her body and never come back. I command that she have a normal cycle each month from this day forward."

Immediately, the pains stopped and she has never had a problem with any monthly cycle since. God performed a miracle, another example of faith in action.

When my children were small, one day I was washing clothes. I absent-mindedly left the bleach on the floor with the top off. As soon as my back was turned, two of my boys decided to take a drink from the bottle. Alfred poured out some bleach into the cap and gave it to Malcolm. As he started to drink it, I heard coughing and spitting. I ran to see what was wrong. I asked Alfred what was wrong with Malcolm. He told me he gave Malcolm a drink of bleach.

"You did what?" I said.

"He said he wanted a drink and I gave it to him," Alfred answered.

"Oh, my God," I said. "What am I going to do?"

I started running around in circles. I snatched up the child to take him to Grady Hospital, but I had no way to get there. I went to my next door neighbor's house, but no one was home. Then the scripture came to me from Mark 16:17-18, particularly verse 18. "They shall take up serpents, and if they drink any deadly thing it shall not hurt them: they shall lay hands on the sick and they shall recover."

I gave the boy a drink of water, then anointed his head with oil, laid hands on him, rebuked the devil in the name of Jesus, and declared healing according to the scripture. I opened his mouth. There was no sign of any damage in his mouth or even the smell of bleach. I began to praise God for His miracle-working power. It was another miracle of faith in action.

In 1984, I was diagnosed with a fibroid tumor by Dr. Crawford W. Long. After giving me a thorough examination and a sonogram test, he told me the tumor was the size of a large grapefruit. It was ripe and needed to come out. He wanted me to think about it and make up my mind what I wanted to do. I began to talk to God. I prayed and had others pray for me.

One Saturday morning, while my husband and I were still lying in bed, I heard a loud, very clear voice speak to me. "I am the Lord thy God that healeth thee, according to Exodus 15:26."

I sat up. "Did you hear what the Lord just said to me?" I asked my husband.

He said he didn't hear anything. It was so loud and clear, I thought he surely must have heard it, but apparently, the Lord was talking only to me.

I told my husband I was not going to have the surgery. The word of the Lord was my confirmation. I knew if God spoke a thing, it would come to pass. My complete healing did not come as an instant miracle, but the tumor shrank until it was gone. It completely dissolved and I have never had any problem with tumors since. Praise God for faith in action.

One Friday morning, I was at work at the Head Start offices. All the staff was called in for a meeting. I walked in and sat in a chair. It didn't appear anything was wrong with me, but after the meeting when I started to get up I found I was unable to stand.

The secretary, Ms. M. Simmons, noticed and stated, "Oh, your feet have probably gone to sleep. Just work them. Shake them and you should be alright."

There was very little I could do. It appeared my feet were disjoined from my legs. Others tried to help me by massaging them, but it didn't help. I sat and prayed, asking the Lord to allow me to make it home.

As the time drew nearer for me to leave for the day, the Lord blessed me to be able to get up and walk to the bus stop. As soon as I got home, the problem started again. I went to bed, wondering what was wrong with me. When I needed to use the bathroom, unless someone was near enough to help, I had to crawl there. For three days I wrestled with this problem.

On Monday, everyone had to go to work and school, and I was left at home alone. No one had offered to take me to a doctor or to the hospital, so I began to cry and have a pity party. While I was lying there, crying, the voice of the Lord began to speak to me through the Twenty-seventh Psalm. I was reading and mediated on that anointed Psalm of David. The first verse spoke to me about my condition and how I would be raised up from my sick bed.

"I, the Lord, am your light and salvation. Whom shall you fear?

The Lord is the strength of your life. Of whom shall you be afraid?" He said to me, "You have been trying to walk in your strength and your strength has failed you. Get up out of that bed, put on your shoes," which I had been too afraid to do, "and begin to walk in my strength. See if you don't make it, because my strength won't fail you."

I got up, as the Lord had spoken, put on my shoes, put away the pity party, and began to walk in Jesus' strength. And His strength did not fail me. I have been walking ever since.

Satan tried to stop me. He kept telling me, "You are going to fall. Your legs are going to give way."

I kept telling that devil I was not walking in my strength. It was Jesus' strength I was walking in, and His strength never fails. I started toward the laundry room, carrying my clothes basket up and down the steps, to and from the basement. The more the devil talked, the more I defeated him, letting him know I was moving in Jesus' strength. I told Satan if he didn't leave me alone I would get on the bus and go to downtown Atlanta.

"You will fall out downtown and no one will be there to help you," the devil taunted.

Guess what? I went downtown and made it back without a fall, walking in the strength of Jesus. I have claimed His word ever since and still walk in His strength without a stick, walker, or wheelchair. Later, I learned the diagnosis for the condition was Gout. Praise God for His miracle-working power of faith in action.

I had a big mole on the back of my neck. When I combed my

hair it would get in the way. Talking to another sister, she told me how she had a mole on her face and anointed it for nine days and it left. So I said, "Lord, if you did it for her, you can do it for me." I began anointing the mole each day in the name of Jesus.

Before I reached the ninth day, the mole had disappeared. I don't even know when it happened, but I praise God for His miracle-working power with faith in action.

I was on duty at work as a nurse's assistant assisting a male patient with a bath. That Sunday I was the only nurse's assistant on duty with eleven patients needing care. The man was tied to the bed. He became agitated and started jerking against me, causing me to get hurt. Ligaments were torn in my neck and my back was injured.

I prayed that God would give me a very good orthopedist. Dr. Hamilton E. Holmes was over Emory and was one of the best orthopedic doctors known. He diagnosed my condition and allowed me the maximum treatment period. I went in and out of therapy for four years. Then finally he told me nothing else could be done for me. I just needed to retire. After all that therapy, I was still unable to sit for long periods of time, unable to lift over eighteen pounds, unable to reach over my head, unable to bend or stoop too long, unable to drive my car over thirty minutes.

One day I was lying on the sofa bed in my living room thinking about what a healer Jesus was and how I didn't need to spend the rest of my life like that. I said, "Lord, I know you can heal me."

The Lord brought Pastor Franklin Walden to my mind. "Go to Conyers, Georgia, to Victory Tabernacle Church and have Pastor Walden pray for you."

That would be just a little bit more than a thirty-minute drive. The devil immediately said, "You can't drive that far with your neck problem."

"'I can do all things through Christ which strengthens me' (Philippians 4:13)," I told him. "Satan, I will be going."

So I drove to Conyers to Victory Tabernacle Church. I got in the prayer line and told Pastor Walden what was wrong and how I needed healing for my neck and back. He told me to sit on the platform and stretch out my legs because when a person had back problems one leg would be shorter than the other. I did what he told me and saw for myself that one leg was shorter.

When he prayed, God performed a miracle. The shorter leg grew out to the length of the other one. He also prayed for my neck. It healed gradually and I was able to get back to work. I started a new job as a counselor for the homeless. Praise God for another miracle, and for faith in action.

I had a bad acid reflux problem. I was in church one Sunday morning in 2000 when a brother called Elder Nelms spoke a word of prophesy about my condition. He said someone was present that whenever they ate their food would stop right in their chest. I knew that was me he was talking about. The acid reflux was so severe sometimes I wondered if I was having a heart attack.

When the elder spoke the word that God was going to heal me, I jumped up and received my healing. I have been healed from acid reflux ever since. Praise God for his miracle-working power.

Come unto me, all ye that labour and are heavy laden, and I will give you rest. Take my yoke upon you, and learn of me; for I am meek and lowly in heart: and ye shall find rest unto your souls. For my yoke is easy, and my burden is light.

Matthew 11:28-30 (KJV)

CHAPTER

3

Jesus' Providing Power

Come unto me, all ye that labour and are heavy laden, and I will give you rest. Take my yoke upon you, and learn of me; for I am meek and lowly in heart: and ye shall find rest unto your souls. For my yoke is easy, and my burden is light.

Matthew 11:28-30 (KJV)

Through many trials and experiences walking with God, I have discovered Him to be Jehovah Jireh: The Lord Will Provide." This name reveals God's ability and willingness to provide for all the needs of His people. God manifested Himself as Jehovah Jireh to Abraham by providing a ram to sacrifice in the place of his son, Isaac, and to Moses by sending food into the wilderness for the children of Israel. He revealed Himself to Elijah as Jehovah Jireh by sending an angel to bring him food and water. In this chapter you will read testimonies that prove my entire life He has been Jehovah Jireh, my provider.

As our wedding date approached, for several weeks my fiancé and I had been looking for an apartment. We had not been able to find one anywhere in the area we wanted. Our time was running out. We had only one week left. We didn't want to change our wedding date so we decided we would just stay with relatives until we found the right place. Several people had offered us a room in their house, but we really wanted a place of our own.

My sister, Mildred who I was staying with at the time, said, "Let's get on our knees and pray you will find an apartment. There is nothing too hard for God."

When we finished our prayer, we felt confident God would give us an answer. Before we even got off our knees, the phone ring. It was my fiancé. He was calling to let us know he had just found an apartment. What a tremendous relief and another of God's powerful blessings. Praise God for a miracle of faith in action.

My husband and I didn't earn much money, so we needed some good credit to buy furniture we needed. Early in our marriage an in-law had signed for us to get bedroom and living room suits for our apartment. But as the family grew, we saw the need for additional furniture. While my husband was at work, I went to several furniture stores to look for the pieces we needed. All of them turned us down due to my husband's poor credit from ten years earlier. I went to one of the stores, Henderson Furniture, at least three times.

I decided to go on a fast for three days, asking God to break this curse on our family. "We are both saved and trying to live for You," I said. "You have forgiven him, and the debt doesn't even exist anymore. Give us a clearance and a clean slate. Allow some store to give us a chance to prove ourselves."

When I came off the fast, I asked God, "Where must I go to apply for furniture?"

"Go back to Henderson Furniture," He said.

"Lord," I replied, "I can't go back there."

"Yes, go back," He said, "but this time ask to speak to the manager."

So I went back to Henderson and asked to speak to the manager. I told him who I was and shook his hand. I said I had been here several times before to get furniture and each time our application had been denied due to my husband's old credit.

"What was the name?" he asked.

I told him, and he pulled our file. He looked at it. "I don't see why you were denied," he said. "That was ten years ago, too far in the past to hold against someone. I'm going to give you all another chance. Go out there and get whatever you want."
I picked out the furniture I needed.

I was always on time with the payments. Later, Henderson Furniture gave us a #1 credit rating. God performed a miracle and we have never had a problem with credit since. That was another example of faith in action.

Once I went to the store and bought two bags of groceries. Traveling home on the city bus, when I reached my destination, I made a mistake and left one of the bags where I had been sitting. So I waited on the other side of the street, waiting for the bus to return, praying my groceries would still be there.

The devil tried to discourage me saying, "You know those groceries are gone. Someone has taken them by now for sure." But I rebuked the devil and stood on faith.

When the bus returned I told the driver I had left a bag of groceries and wanted to get it. The bus driver allowed me to get on the bus and find my groceries. There they were. I praise God for victory with faith in action.

At one of the jobs the Lord blessed me with, each year at the same time I would get a pay increase. That particular year, though my evaluation had been very good, the usual raise time had come and gone with no change. Wondering about my expected raise, I began to pray. One Monday morning when I walked in the door I said, "Satan, in the name of Jesus, loose my money."

The very same day I was told I would get my pay raise in Friday's check. Praise God for another miracle through faith in action.

For years, my husband and I reared our children living in Atlanta housing projects. I began to pray and ask God to give me the kind of job that would enable us to save money to get out of the projects yet still be at home to be with the children when they came in from school, one close enough that I could walk to work.

Jesus led me to go to the Eventide Elderly Home across the street. Praying, I asked the supervisor if they were hiring. She replied that they did have a position. It was a split shift for dining and kitchen work, serving the boarders and cleaning up from 7:30 a.m. to 2:00 p.m. then from 5:00 p.m. to 7:00 p.m. This was just what I was looking for.

I was supposed to work every other Sunday, but I told the supervisor my husband was the Sunday school superintendent at our church so my children needed to be in Sunday school and I needed to be there with them if at all possible. God began to work in my favor. The supervisor granted my wishes. I went to the housing office to inform the manager I had started working. In government housing, when your income changes your rent goes up accordingly. I told the manager I had started working because it was our plan to move out as soon as possible.

"Mrs. Zackery," he said, "if you are planning to move, I'm sure you will need that little finance to help with moving expenses. Just keep it to yourself and I hope the best for you all."

That was another example of God's miracle-working power, faith in action.

My husband and I started looking for a house. We had in mind a brick house with four bedrooms or three bedrooms with a basement. A realtor was taking us to see many houses around the city of Decatur and also in Atlanta. We were unable to find any we could agree on. When I told people I wanted a brick house not over twenty thousand dollars, they thought I was crazy.

When it looked as if it wasn't going to happen it was a little hard for me to hold onto my faith. We were about to give up, but while I continued to think about it and pray, knowing what miracles God had already performed for us in the past, I told my husband, "I'm going to try one more realtor." I called Reese Realty and told Juanita Reese what kind of house we were looking for and the price.

"I have two houses I can show you," Ms. Reese replied. "I will show you the one at 29 Arlington Dr., NW first."

When she drove up to that house, before I got out of the car, I said, "This is it."

To this day I don't know what the other house looked like or where it was located. Ms. Reese showed us around the property. It was a three-bedroom ranch-style brick house with a full basement selling for twenty thousand dollars. The owner even left a double oven, a gas range, a refrigerator, a window air conditioner, a washing machine and dryer, and drapes in the living room. He asked only five hundred dollars for all those items. Praise God for His miracle-working power and faith in action.

The Lord began to speak to my spirit about doing social work. I didn't know how I could get a job as a social worker, but I went to different worksites and employment agencies inquiring about positions. They would ask if I had a Master's degree in social work. I would say no and be told a Master's degree was required for that position.

So I went back to God, praying, "Lord, you told me to get a job in this field, but I am being turned away everywhere I inquire." I began doing volunteer work at my youngest child's Head Start center. Soon some positions became available for para-professionals to work under the center director. There were eleven positions, and I was one of sixty people who applied.

I was working temporarily at a boarding house for the elderly, filling in for a woman who was ill. I was cooking for the boarders and everyone seemed to like my cooking. The owner was very pleased with my work. She was telling all her friends what a wonderful cook I was, including the lady in whose place I was working. Though she was quite sick, but she persuaded the owner to let me go so she could return to work. Without saying anything to me about it, the owner promised to let her come back the following Monday. So that Friday when she paid me she told me she would not need me anymore. Since she didn't explain anything to me, I was really surprised and puzzled. No one had ever just "let me go" like that.

The word of God came to comfort me. Roman 8:28 promises, "And we know that all things work together for good to them that love God, to them who are called according to His purpose."

In my kitchen on Monday morning, my phone rang. It was Mrs. Mamie Simmons at the Head Start center where I had put in an application for a para-professional position. She informed me that interviews for those positions would be Wednesday night. Of the sixty people that had applied for the eleven positions, I came out number fifteen, which allowed me to be interviewed again. She said letters had been sent to inform candidates of the interviews, but I hadn't received one. I began to see that God works in mysterious ways! If the woman at the boarding home had not let me go on that Friday, I would not have been home on Monday to get the call for the Wednesday night interview.

I was hired with the agency, Economic Opportunity of Atlanta for the Head Start program. EOA provided the training we needed through Georgia State University and other state agencies to become skilled counselors and interviewers. However, we were not aware the jobs were funded for only one year.

I knew God had chosen me and performed a miracle to get me that job. I never knew about the short funding until my coworkers who were hired the same time I was were let go. The agency was allowed to keep only one person to work with the social service administrator and I was chosen. The Lord blessed me to move up into that position and even to a supervisor position for six months when they were without a coordinator. I worked on that job for fourteen years.

During that time, I helped train many other social service assistants and college students doing intern hours. I became one of the best caseworkers in the agency. I was called upon to work with the worst cases. Praise God for His miracle-working power for another example of faith in action.

When I left EOA, not working for a while, it was hard for me to find another job. I tried several places, but was not successful. I began to pray and asked others to pray for me. Then a friend told me to go to the Task Force for the Homeless and put in an application for a counselor position. I applied, but didn't hear anything back from them. She also advised me to apply to the Atlanta Urban League Senior program, so I went and signed up.

When Pamela interviewed me, she wanted to know what type of work I'd like. I said I wanted office work or counseling if possible because that was what I had been doing. I told her I was a people person so I enjoyed human services work. I said I would also like to get some computer skills.

"I know just the place," Pamela said. "I'm going to send you where you can get good on-the-job office training even on the computer—the Task Force for the Homeless. Though I didn't tell her, I began to praise God within myself because I had already applied there. I knew God was getting my foot in the door.

So I went and interviewed with Wendy and Anita Beaty. They

welcomed me aboard. I mentioned the application I had put in with the Task Force and they reminded me I had six months to work as a volunteer through Atlanta Urban League.

When the six months were up I was not offered a job with the Task Force. Ms. Ethel Kit, supervisor of Atlanta Urban League Senior Program, threatened to pull me away if they didn't hire me because she knew I was doing good work. My supervisor at the Task Force got busy talking to his supervisor and stated that he didn't want to lose me and wasn't going to let me go. That's how God performed a miracle again. The Task Force hired me September 2, 1995, six months after I had come on board as a volunteer, March 1, 1995.

Fifteen years later, I'm still working with the agency. I believed God for that job and I praise God for faith in action.

On the last job God gave me, there was a delay about a pay raise. My supervisor gave me a very good evaluation and recommended that I should get an increase, but there was no response from the program director. After working there thirteen months, I asked God what I should do. How should I approach the situation?

The Lord led me to write a letter to the executive director, and He told me exactly what to say in the letter. She responded by agreeing verbally to give me an increase of about fifteen-hundred dollars. Praise God for his miracle-working power with faith in action.

Later, I prayed again when I thought I should get another pay increase, and without saying a word, I was given a four-thousand-dollar raise. God spoke to them for me. Praise God for His miracle-working power and faith in action.

After a couple years, my work load increased because I was doing two jobs with one single pay. So I decided to write a letter and state that I would like to talk to the directors about being overworked and underpaid, holding down two jobs. No one would come out or call a meeting with me, but praise God; they gave me a nice pay increase. Praise God for His miracle-working power with faith in action.

On that same job, the executive director was conducting a staff meeting. She went around the table asking each person, one by one, what they had to say. But when she got to me the question changed. Instead of asking what I had to say, she asked, "Juanita, what do you need?"

"I need money," I replied.

I told her I had not given any thought to or planned what I would say. So when we walked out of the meeting she followed me and, to my surprise, asked, "What is your salary?"

I told her and she said, "I am going to give you a four-thousand-dollar increase. I was shocked and began to praise God for His miracle-working power with faith in action.

I had been praying, asking God to allow me to get my house paid off and all my other debts cleared before the end of 2008. I had no idea how that would happen. I couldn't see it with the natural eye.

Without my knowing anything about it, the Lord had been using my children to plan something special for me.

I prayed and asked God to allow me to get my house paid off again and all my other debts cleared up before the end of 2008. I had no idea how this would happen. I couldn't see any of these things with a natural eye. The Lord had been using my children to plan a big 70th birthday for me and I didn't know anything about it. On my birthday, August 22, 2008 they gave me a fish fry along with cake, ice cream, and some small gifts. Seven of my children came and no friends.

My son Alfred told me a limousine would pick me up the next day and take me to a hotel for dinner. He told me to pack my luggage, so I could spend the night. When I got to the hotel, it was a big surprise party with seven of my children, many relatives, many old friends and old co-workers. They planned a great menu with four meats, variety of vegetables, desserts, and beverages. I received several cards, gifts, and a well-organized program. Seven children and all eleven grandchildren participated in the program. At the end of the program, I was presented with a check for $10,000.00, given to me by my eight children. I used the money along with money from a Roth IRA to pay off my house note, my visa credit card, and I did some repair work on my house. Praise God for his miracle working power and another faith in action.

When I First Sought Jesus by Juanita Collier Zackery

When I first sought the savior I told Him in my prayer,

"Lord, if you can just save me, I'll own you anywhere."

I tarried and I tarried, all night long. I cried, I prayed, and repented,

But my soul just couldn't be contented.

Then about three weeks and four days, in God's own time,

The Holy Ghost came and moved me around.

Then I began to speak in a tongue unknown

And I knew for sure, I was truly reborn.

My father, who was lacking of Grace, wanted to know what it was I had,

What made me want to jump and jerk so bad.

With the grace of God down in my soul, I politely told, I had the gift of the Holy Ghost.

About the Author

Juanita Collier Zackery was born in Macon County, Montezuma, Georgia, on August 22, 1938, to the late Walter Collier and Elberta Collier. The seventh child, she became the third of the siblings to complete a high school education. Shortly after graduating, she moved to Atlanta to live with her oldest sister, Mildred. Both became employed at the Varsity, the legendary drive-in eatery located near the Georgia Tech campus. Two years later, at the age of twenty-one, she met and married Grady Zackery. She eventually gave birth to eight children, four boys and four girls.

She pursued education in the field of social services and for fourteen years served as a social service counselor with the Head Start program in Atlanta. She also received training in patient sitting and earned certification as a nurse's assistant, working in that field for a few years. Being a confirmed people person, she eagerly embraced human services positions. She spent fourteen years as a paid walk-in coordinator and counselor for the Task Force for the Homeless.

She has served more than three years as an unpaid volunteer counselor for the homeless. A widow for twenty-one years and a "mother" in the church, she enjoys ministering to inmates in various prison facilities.

With her first book, I Learned to Lean on Jesus with Faith in Action, she continues her person-to-person lifestyle in the hope that it will be a blessing to all who read it.

www.ingramcontent.com/pod-product-compliance
Lightning Source LLC
Chambersburg PA
CBHW031530040426
42445CB00009B/464